# ACRES *of* DIAMONDS

## PARTICIPANT'S GUIDE

# ACRES *of* DIAMONDS

## PARTICIPANT'S GUIDE

DISCOVERING GOD'S BEST RIGHT WHERE YOU ARE

# JENTEZEN FRANKLIN

**Chosen**
*a division of Baker Publishing Group*
Minneapolis, Minnesota

Published by Chosen Books
11400 Hampshire Avenue South
Bloomington, Minnesota 55438
www.chosenbooks.com

Chosen Books is a division of
Baker Publishing Group, Grand Rapids, Michigan

Printed in the United States of America

ISBN 978-0-8007-9962-5

Unless otherwise indicated, Scripture quotations are from the New King James Version®. Copyright © 1982 by Thomas Nelson. Used by permission. All rights reserved.

Where indicated, Scripture quotations taken from the New English Bible, copyright © Cambridge University Press and Oxford University Press 1961, 1970. All rights reserved.

Cover design by LOOK Design Studio

Author is represented by The Fedd Agency, Inc.

20   21   22   23   24   25   26      7   6   5   4   3   2   1

# Contents

# A Note from Jentezen

Often we think the key to success lies somewhere "out there"—in the great beyond just outside of reach. If we could only get there, we would have what we need to satisfy our deepest longings. But in Christ, we have everything we need right where we are. When we begin to see, value and grow what we have, here and now, we will uncover acres of diamonds beneath our feet.

In 1869, near the banks of the Tigris River, Russell Conwell found himself on the back of a camel. Conwell was an attorney, and he had once attended Yale; now he was the captive audience to his Arab guide, who was especially fond of telling stories—thousands of them, it seemed. One story in particular, however, caught Conwell's attention.

The guide told of a man called Ali Hafed, who owned a large farm. Ali Hafed worked hard for everything he had, and in many ways he was blessed and content—until, that is, an old priest came to visit. The priest told Ali Hafed about the discovery of diamonds, of which the farmer was astounded and curious. The next day, Ali Hafed was so desperate to find diamonds that he decided to leave everything behind and begin the search. He sold his farm, hugged his wife and his kids good-bye and set out to find these rare gems. In time, he promised his family, he would come back a wealthy man.

Ali Hafed journeyed to East Africa. No diamonds. He went to Palestine. No diamonds. He went to Europe. No diamonds. Finally, after spending all of his money in search of great fortune, the farmer wandered into Spain. Still, no diamonds. There, Ali Hafed reached a point of such despair that he decided to end his life. He jumped into a raging river, never to be seen again.

One day, the man who bought Ali Hafed's farm found a unique stone on his new property. He found it so beautiful that he decided to display it on his mantel as a decoration. The next day, the same priest who had told Ali Hafed about diamonds stopped by. Noticing the stone on the mantel, he exclaimed, "That's a diamond!"

The farmer didn't believe him, but the stone was, in fact, a diamond. The farmer showed the priest the stream in which he found the stone, and the two of them discovered countless more just like the one on the mantel.

The man who had bought the farm from Ali Hafed had inadvertently discovered the diamond mine of Golconda, the most magnificent diamond mine in history. In fact, crown jewels worn by royalty all over the world, including the Queen Mother in England, come from this very mine—from the same land, the same garden, and the same stream that Ali Hafed had left behind.

This story became part of a speech that Conwell was asked to give 6,152 times in his life, a fact included in *Ripley's Believe It or Not!* He eventually turned it into a book, *Acres of Diamonds*, which became a bestseller. The book tells of Ali Hafed and others who illustrate the same point: Instead of dreaming of fortune elsewhere, we ought to pay attention to opportunities that lie right in front of us.

Conwell shares another story about a farmer in Pennsylvania. Upon hearing about the discovery of oil in Canada, this man became an expert in the subject of collecting coal oil from streams. He eventually sold his farm for $833 and went to work for his cousin in Canada, doing the job he'd trained himself to do. Not long after, the man who bought his farm discovered coal oil in a brook on the property, worth, back then, one hundred million dollars. The self-taught "expert" had failed to recognize the deposits of coal oil on his own land.

Ali Hafed and the farmer from Pennsylvania left where they were to try to find what they had all along. They never uncovered the potential of the place they were planted. They never even suspected they had been living on acres of diamonds.

8

Many people are discontent with where they are. They leave their marriages, their jobs, their churches, their dreams in search of a better marriage, job, church or dream.

Do you believe you have to go somewhere else to find what you think will make you happy? You don't! Whether you realize it or not, if you know Jesus, you are living on acres of diamonds. God's best is right here, right now. If He has called you to a place or to a relationship, unless He has released you from that situation, you must stay. Even if it's hard. Even if you don't like it. Even if you think nothing can come from it. The grass isn't greener somewhere else. I promise you this. You just have to learn to see, value and grow what you have, where you are.

We must take the posture of the psalmist who asked God to "open my eyes, that I may see wondrous things from Your law" (Psalm 119:18). The implication in this verse is that wonderful things might be all around you, but your eyes are closed. You cannot see them. You may think you are living in spiritual poverty, when you are actually surrounded by untold spiritual wealth. Our vision is clearer when we ask God to open our eyes.

When we believe that what we need to make us happy is anywhere other than where God has us, we will never see His best for our lives, our very own acres of diamonds.

It takes three things to make a diamond: time, intense heat and extreme pressure. It doesn't come easily or quickly. What does this mean to you? The hard times you are going through serve a purpose. God is putting on the pressure and turning up the heat so that He can bring forth a diamond. But it can only happen if you stop running and stay put.

I want to encourage you through the next six sessions to be open to what God can teach you, show you or change in you right here, right now. I want you to learn how to dig in your own backyard and open your eyes to the best God has in store for you.

Don't undervalue where you are right now. God didn't leave you without potential. He didn't leave you without opportunity. As you work through this study on your own or with a small group, ask Him to open your eyes to the wonderful things that are all around you. No matter how hopeless or painful your situation is right now, God can do amazing things in and through you. He will uncover His best for you.

# How to Use This Guide

You can work through this participant's guide in a group setting or on your own. It is also formatted to work in conjunction with my book *Acres of Diamonds* and the accompanying DVD teaching. But don't worry if you haven't read the book or won't get a chance to watch the video segments. There is plenty of content that will help you begin, today, to discover God's best for you in your life, in your trials, in your workplace and in your relationships.

This participant's guide is divided into six sessions that each include the following:

- A big idea to introduce the overall message of the session
- A start-up segment that sets the stage for the video session and the discussion to follow
- Video teaching notes and an outline
- A set of in-depth group discussion questions drawn from the video, the Bible, my book and real-life matters
- A closing prayer
- A reflection and action segment to be completed on your own time

If you want to dive deeper and maximize your experience outside of your small group, spend time in the "Personal Reflection" and "Personal Action" portions at the end of each session. There are some things you may not be ready to share with others or those in your small group, so you can use this segment in a more private manner as well as in a more practical way. I encourage you to take this opportunity to reflect on what you have learned and on what God has been speaking to you about.

## What You'll Need

Unless otherwise marked, all the Scripture references in this guide are offered in the New King James Version (NKJV). If you prefer a different version, have a Bible or Bible app handy to look up the verses in the translation of your choice. While not necessary, as space is provided in this guide, consider using a journal or digital device to jot down notes or anything that speaks to you. Finally, while you don't have to, you'll get the most out of this guide if you read my book *Acres of Diamonds*.

Follow the schedule below to coordinate with this participant's guide:

| Read | Watch | Discuss |
|---|---|---|
| Introduction and chapters 1, 2 and 3 of *Acres of Diamonds* | Video session 1 | Session 1, "The Power of Staying Right Where You Are Right Now" |
| Chapters 4 and 5 | Video session 2 | Session 2, "Open My Eyes" |
| Chapters 6, 7 and 8 | Video session 3 | Session 3, "Grow Deep Roots to Bear Fruit Up" |
| Chapter 9 | Video session 4 | Session 4, "Work Is Worship" |
| Chapter 10 | Video session 5 | Session 5, "How to Be a Hero" |
| Chapters 11 and 12 | Video session 6 | Session 6, "Live Now in the Light of Eternity" |

I'm excited to see how God is going to uncover acres of diamonds in your life.

# The Power of Staying Right Where You Are Right Now

> **Big Idea for This Session**
>
> The acres of diamonds of God's best are found when you obey His command to stay here and release your faith now, knowing that whatever your situation, He will work it out for good.

## Session Start-Up

There is something powerful in where you are right now. Your treasure is in today. When we focus on what's ahead or what's behind, we will miss the power of now! We allow today to be crucified between yesterday and tomorrow. I like to say that yesterday is a cashed check, tomorrow is a promissory note and today is cash in the hand. Now matters. Today. This moment. It's time to smile. It's time to laugh. It's time to live. Yes, even when it seems impossible.

We cannot keep waiting for the perfect time to do or change something—there is no greater time than now. If you are waiting on a miracle, stop waiting and believe for it now. If you'd like to change bad habits, stop making excuses and work on them now. If you are planning to spend more time with your family when work settles down, don't wait. Start doing it now. Don't keep looking down the road, saying, "Someday . . .," and letting today pass you by.

Sometimes the greatest miracle God will do comes during the most inopportune time. It happens because only in His power will we ever be able to pull it off. When you feel God leading you somewhere or toward something, in these moments, you have to see the diamonds right where you are—not the stress, not the stretch, not the excuses, not the difficulties and not the impossibilities.

The word *now* spelled backwards is *won*. Here's some truth: The battle is already won, even if we cannot see it with our natural eyes. This is why we praise God now, not when we see change in our circumstance. We trust God now, not when we understand everything. We must choose to believe God now, not when the manifestation comes. That is what faith is. The Bible puts it like this: "Now faith is the substance of things hoped for, the evidence of things not seen" (Hebrews 11:1). The definition of faith is not someday. Faith *is*. It's now.

If you are looking at the field of your life right now, you may feel discouraged. Financial stress. Health problems. Family conflict. Depression. Anxiety. All of these things may cloud your vision and daunt your faith.

Remember that diamonds are formed in time and with intense heat and extreme pressure. The acres of diamonds that lie underneath the surface of your life are created in the same way. There is a reason for the heat. There is a reason for the pressure. So, today, even right now, be encouraged. When we face problems, trials and adversity, God already has a plan in place to bring victory out of that situation.

This is why we don't run from the difficult times. We don't quit. We don't give up. You might not understand everything you are going through in this moment. You might not have all the answers to all your questions. But unless you persevere through the hardships, you'll never receive the gifts, the blessings, the diamonds that God will bring forth through them.

We don't know what God is doing behind the scenes as our stories unfold. So when He calls us to a place or to a marriage, we stay. We learn to be obedient. Hard places lead to high places. God does not look for perfect places for you to flourish. He works in surprising places.

Commit to staying right where you are. You are on the right track. Stay right where He has you planted. It may be a great challenge to stay and see what God has for you right where you are, but it also brings the greater reward.

## Talk about It

When was the last time you thought about leaving a job, a church, a community or a relationship? Why?

## Session 1 Video

*Watch video session 1. While viewing the video, use the outline and spaces below to record key ideas or any thoughts you want to remember.*

### Video Teaching Notes

Appreciate and understand the value of where God has you right now.

Get on God's clock.

"My times are in Your hand" (Psalm 31:15).

_____

_____

_____

God is doing a work in you while you wait.

_____

_____

_____

When you understand that everything you're going through is preparing you for where He is taking you, you'll discover God's best right where you are.

_____

_____

_____

God will use your seed, your time and your harvest.

_____

_____

_____

"While the earth remains, seedtime and harvest, cold and heat, winter and summer, and day and night shall not cease" (Genesis 8:22).

_____

_____

_____

God knows what's involved in bringing a diamond out of you.

A diamond is perfected through heat, pressure and time.

### Video Discussion

Name one thing that struck you or that you learned, experienced or gained from this video teaching.

## Small-Group Discussion

1. In the video teaching, I make the point that God's timing is not our timing. To get the most out of where we are, we must get on His clock and off of ours. What does this mean to you? What is the danger in living life based on your timing?

2. There is a temptation to live in the past and believe things can never be as good as they were. It is also easy to focus on what may (or may not) happen in the future. What are you holding on to from the past or hoping for in the future that keeps you from enjoying or appreciating the present?

3. God works in unusual places. Barren places. Low places. Places of intense heat and pressure. Lazarus was resurrected four days after he died, smelling of rot and decay. God found Moses in the desert, Job in the trial and three Hebrew young men in the fiery

furnace. Share an unusual place where God found and worked in you, uncovering acres of diamonds.

4. Peter writes in 1 Peter 4:12–13,

> Beloved, do not think it strange concerning the fiery trial which is to try you, as though some strange thing happened to you; but rejoice to the extent that you partake of Christ's sufferings, that when His glory is revealed, you may also be glad with exceeding joy.

Why do you think many of us are surprised when hard times come? How does having a mindset of accepting the inevitability of trials benefit us?

5. In the video teaching, I offer that we are made better in trials and stronger through our afflictions. Share an instance when you have grown spiritually, physically, emotionally or mentally in a trial or affliction.

6. In what place or relationship has God called you to stay? Is your situation meeting or falling short of your expectations? What can you do to allow God to work in His power and in His time to uncover His best?

7. In *Acres of Diamonds* (p. 58) I write,

> Sometimes it is better to go through your worst day where God wants you than your best day anywhere else. It is easy to think that God is going to do something great in distant places, but He can do a mighty work in a dust bowl. When it looks like your dream or your resources are drying up, God will be with you. And He will help you.

How does this encourage you if you are in a season of famine?

## Bonus Questions

8. Name something in your life you've been putting off but you're ready to do now.

9. Describe a time when you have seen God's glory unfold in His timing rather than your own. How did it differ from and even exceed your expectations?

10. If you are exactly where God wants you, what might you miss if you aren't "all in" in this place?

## Wrap-Up

Today we have learned that sometimes God calls us to stay in a place that looks like a dust bowl. With our natural eyes, we may not see Him at work. But He is. In time, He will uncover acres of diamonds in a place of famine, pain or failure. Release your faith in this very moment and believe it!

Let's close this time together in prayer. Here are some ideas from this session that can guide your conversation with God:

- Thank God that He is the same yesterday, today and forever, and that He will never be greater in your life than He is right now.
- Ask Him to help you cultivate joy unspeakable in your life, even if you are going through a trial.
- Ask the Holy Spirit to reveal areas in your life in which you may be tempted to run, give up or go somewhere else.
- Offer to God your commitment to stay planted wherever He has called you.

## Prepare for the Next Session

Before the group meets again, read chapters 4 and 5 in *Acres of Diamonds*.

## BETWEEN SESSIONS

### Personal Reflection

If God is in the process of creating a diamond in you, Psalm 1:1–3 offers great insight on what to do when you stay right where you are:

> Blessed is the man who walks not in the counsel of the ungodly, nor stands in the path of sinners, nor sits in the seat of the scornful; but his delight is in the law of the LORD, and in His law he meditates day and night. He shall be like a tree planted by the rivers of water, that brings forth its fruit in its season, whose leaf also shall not wither; and whatever he does shall prosper.

The author of this passage talks about the importance of meditating on God's Word. I like to call this "self-talk." Think about some of the things you have been saying or thinking that may not be encouraging or helpful in your current situation—things like *I don't think I'm ever going to get through this* or *This obstacle is impossible to overcome.*

Take some time to reflect on some of your favorite Scriptures that can encourage and remind you that God will give you the grace and strength to handle, in His power, every situation that comes your way.

## Personal Action

Sometimes life does not turn out exactly how we want it to. And because life hurts or seems unfair, we long to rush through the season we're in (or pray to skip it altogether) instead of seeking God and His purposes in our storms. I am not saying this is easy or that it comes naturally, but it is important to do if He is to uncover His best for our lives.

I want you to write down five things that you can do right now to remind yourself to be present in this very moment. But first, I want you to take a deep breath. Then another. And another. When you are mindful of the very breath God has given you, it will help to calm your spirit and quiet your mind. Psalm 46:10 gives us good advice: "Be still, and know that I am God." Before you write down those five action items, take a few minutes to quiet yourself in His presence. Right now, no matter where you are, no matter what your situation, remember, God is with you.

# 2

# Open My Eyes

> **Big Idea for This Session**
>
> When you are walking through the dark hallway of life's pressures and trials, God can open your eyes to discover untapped potential, beauty, truth and life.

## Session Start-Up

Some of us believe there is something better for us somewhere else. Whether you realize it or not, if you know Jesus, you are living on acres of diamonds. You will find nothing greater in this world than a relationship with Him. You do not have to look somewhere else for peace, purpose and fulfillment. You just have to open your eyes to see what you have right in front of you.

The Prodigal Son learned that lesson the hard way. He thought what he wanted—fun, happiness and fulfillment—could not be found in his father's house. So, like Ali Hafed, he left to search for these things. He never found them. Finally, his eyes opened and he realized his acres of diamonds were actually back home. He came to his senses and went back to his father's house.

There's a story told about a man on a train.\* As he passed dilapidated buildings, he cried, "Wow! Wonderful!" To most, his view wouldn't be described as wonderful. But to a man who had been blind for thirty years and was finally able to see, even the ruins of once-thriving neighborhoods looked wonderful.

Perspective!

When you ask God to open your eyes, things change. Maybe not according to your expectations. You may still find yourself in a dark hallway for a time, but He can give you a new vision even in that place. You can see provision. You can see the right direction. You can see protection. Importantly, you can experience God's presence, particularly in moments you didn't think He was there.

It is said that when God closes one door, He opens another. True, but I have learned it's hell out there in the hallway. It can be hard to have the right perspective when we are going through a difficult period, but this is when it's most critical to ask God to open our eyes to His presence, His grace and His truth.

## Talk about It

How have the trials in your life limited your vision?

## Session 2 Video

*Watch video session 2. While viewing the video, use the outline and spaces below to record key ideas or any thoughts you want to remember.*

### Video Teaching Notes

Enjoy where you are right now.

---

\*Bob Gass and Debby Gass, "Today, Open Your Eyes," *The Word for Today*, March 16, 2016, https://vision.org.au/the-word-for-today/2016/03/16/today-open-your-eyes/.

"Open my eyes, that I may see wondrous things from Your law" (Psalm 119:18).

Live with a spirit of gratitude.

"Look now toward heaven, and count the stars. . . . So shall your descendants be" (Genesis 15:5).

God will open your eyes, even in a desert.

When God is going to do something in your life, He will give you a picture. And if you can see it, you can do it.

The Lord is your doorkeeper.

_____

_____

_____

### Video Discussion

Name one thing that struck you or that you learned, experienced or gained from this video teaching.

## Small-Group Discussion

1. In the video teaching, I talk about when Abraham got into conflict with his nephew Lot, as told in Genesis 13. Abraham gave him a choice of which land to settle. Lot chose the well-watered plains of Jordan, which left Abraham to make his home in a hot and dry desert. It wasn't the greatest or the most fruitful land on which to settle, but in this place God gave Abraham a vision for his life:

   > I will make your descendants as the dust of the earth; so
   > that if a man could number the dust of the earth, then your
   > descendants also could be numbered. Arise, walk in the land
   > through its length and its width, for I give it to you.
   >                                          Genesis 13:16–17

   > Count the stars if you are able to number them . . . so shall
   > your descendants be.
   >                                          Genesis 15:5

   The sand represented Abraham's natural family that would come through Isaac. The stars represented his spiritual family, the body of Christ. God gave Abraham visions that he would become the father of both a spiritual and a natural family. And it happened in a hot and dry desert.

How does this encourage you if you are in what feels like a godforsaken season in your life?

2. Proverbs 17:24 offers great insight on how we can do our part in uncovering God's best: "Wisdom is in the sight of him who has understanding, but the eyes of a fool are on the ends of the earth."

   How does this Scripture apply to your life? Are you seeking wisdom from God or looking out for your own interests somewhere else?

3. Ephesians 1:17–18 tells us,

   > The God of our Lord Jesus Christ, the Father of glory, may give to you the spirit of wisdom and revelation in the knowledge of Him, the eyes of your understanding being enlightened; that you may know what is the hope of His calling, what are the riches of the glory of His inheritance in the saints, and what is the exceeding greatness of His power toward us who believe, according to the working of His mighty power.

   When you look into the mirror of Scripture, your eyes will be enlightened and you will see what God sees. When we faithfully study and meditate on His Word, we begin to change our perception of who we are. God superimposes His image over what we presently think or feel about ourselves.

   What are some perceptions about yourself or your situation that you need to change to better reflect what God says?

4. What keeps you from seeing God's best—acres of diamonds—in your life?

5. In *Acres of Diamonds* (p. 76) I write,

   > You can't get somewhere you can't see. You will not find acres of diamonds until you get a divinely inspired image of what they might look like. You might see where you are as a field of failure, a land of hurt, a home of bitter contention, a

place of disaster. All bad things. You need to get a picture of and meditate on "whatever things are true, whatever things are noble, whatever things are just, whatever things are pure, whatever things are lovely, whatever things are of good report, if there is any virtue and if there is anything praiseworthy" (Philippians 4:8).

God has called you to where you are for a reason. There is a promise there. A purpose. It is time to start turning that into a picture, no matter what your life or your place looks like right now. Remember, pictures are developed in darkrooms.

I discuss this very thing in the video teaching as well. If you can see it, you can do it. Describe a picture of what it might look like when God uncovers acres of diamonds in your life.

6. Talk about a situation in which God opened your eyes and you finally realized that, in trying to do things your own way, you were headed in the wrong direction.

7. Share a time in your life in which you were grateful for something that didn't happen.

## Bonus Questions

8. In Luke 24 we read that after Jesus died and was resurrected, two people were walking on the road to Emmaus. Suddenly, a man appeared and started walking with them. It was Jesus, but He had disguised Himself to appear to be a stranger. The two people started telling Him how discouraged and depressed they were over the fact that their Messiah had died. Without revealing His identity, Jesus started talking about Himself—who He was and how the Savior must suffer these things. Finally, after walking and talking all day long, the two strangers invited Jesus to have supper with them. Jesus accepted. As the three of them sat down to eat, the instant Jesus broke the bread, "their eyes

were opened and they knew Him; and He vanished from their sight" (verse 31).

Talk about a difficult time in which you could feel or sense God's presence with you.

9. Share a time in which God opened a door for you in a dark hallway.

10. Worship is spiritual warfare. No matter how great your pain, your hurt or your sorrow, you can be victorious in battle if you will praise and worship the living God. What role does worship play in your spiritual life? How do you make this a priority?

## Wrap-Up

Today we have learned that our perspective in life can become cloudy when we experience trials and challenges. This is why we must pray daily for God to open our eyes to see His goodness, His vision for us, the acres of diamonds of His best. No matter how much pressure and heat we endure, we can find peace, rest and joy wherever we are planted.

Let's close this time together in prayer. Here are some ideas from this session that can guide your conversation with God:

- Ask your heavenly Father to open your eyes to see your life in a different light.
- Thank Him for the blessings He has generously sown in your life.
- Ask Him for a greater appreciation for what you have right now, whether your health, loving relationships or a good church.
- Pray for God to give you a picture of what He is calling you to do in your circumstance and/or give you the faith to see it through.

## Prepare for the Next Session

Before the group meets again, read chapters 6, 7 and 8 in *Acres of Diamonds*.

# BETWEEN SESSIONS

## Personal Reflection

Tough seasons have a way of stealing our peace. Your mind races all the time. Upsetting thoughts run rampant. Recently, needing a word from God, I was studying the Bible, and I came upon the story of Jesus on the boat with His disciples in the middle of a storm. While the winds raged and the waves tossed the boat around like a rag doll, Jesus was asleep in the stern. Conversely, the disciples were overcome with panic.

Reading this story that I'd read many times, I asked God what He was trying to reveal to me through it. I heard Him in my spirit, saying, *I'm trying to teach you how to rest in a storm. Rest in what I've told you. Rest in what I've promised you. Don't panic—I'm God.*

Rest in the storm.

Peter eventually learned how to do this. In Acts 12, we read how Herod beheaded James, one of the disciples. The evil king seized Peter next and threw him in jail with the intention of killing him later. On the night Peter was scheduled to be executed, an angel came to deliver him from prison. What was Peter doing at the time? Sleeping! Can you imagine? If you knew someone had a hit on you, would you be asleep? I'm not sure I would be. But Peter was. He was so conked out, in fact, the Bible says the angel had to slap him on his side to wake him up!

How could Peter rest in such a time? Earlier in his life, Jesus had prophesied that when Peter was an old man, he was going to be bound and killed (see John 21:18–19). Well, I like to believe Peter remembered that prophecy, and seeing as he wasn't an old man, he knew it wasn't yet time to go, no matter what Herod had schemed.

God is telling you the same thing today. Rest. The blessing is coming. The breakthrough is coming. The acres of diamonds will be uncovered in your life. In a little while, He is going to open up the windows of heaven. He will bring beauty out of ashes. If you stay planted as a tree, you will see how faithful God can be.

Be encouraged, for God brings an end to darkness. You will not be in the dark hallway forever. It has a beginning, and God has a time for it to end.

Read the story of the disciples in the boat in Mark 4:35–41. Meditate on this passage of Scripture. Ask God to speak to you through it. Now write down three ways you can rest in a storm.

## Personal Action

We are in a battle. The enemy seeks to destroy us. Worship is how we invite God to fight our battles for us. When we choose to turn our eyes on the majesty of Jesus and worship Him with our whole hearts, power is released. We experience peace, joy unspeakable and rest.

Worship puts life in the proper perspective. It helps us to see who we are in relation to who God is. Your enemies or circumstances may seem so large and powerful that they are all you can see. When you worship, you reduce the size of everything around you. God becomes your focus. The greatest thing you can do in a personal battle is worship the Lord. It will make a huge difference in your life.

Depression or anxiety may try to drag you down and steal your joy and passion for Jesus. But you weren't created to be bound by this kind of inner turmoil. You were born to worship. You were born to lift your hands and shower your Father in heaven with praise and thanksgiving. When you're walking through darkness, when it seems as though you don't have any answers, when you're confused and don't know what to do, remember that you were born to worship.

Give God glory no matter where you are or what you are going through. When Job experienced hell on earth, his first response was to fall to the ground in worship. It may not have been joyful worship, but he praised the Lord, saying, "Naked I came from my mother's womb, and naked shall I return there. The LORD gave, and the LORD has taken away; blessed be the name of the LORD" (Job 1:21). Even if you've lost everything, you were born to stand in the rubble and ashes and say, "God alone is worthy of glory and honor and praise."

Right now, create some space to worship God. Find a quiet room free of distractions. Put your phone away. Stop thinking about your to-do list. Put on worship music and lift your hands to heaven. Begin to worship God. It doesn't matter if you can sing on key or not. God doesn't require talent to worship. He desires your heart. Spend time worshiping Him for who He is. The darkness in your hallway will decrease as the light of His glory shines forth.

31

# ❖ 3 ❖

# Grow Deep Roots
# to Bear Fruit Up

---

**Big Idea for This Session**

You can't choose what happens to you, but you can choose to let it take you down or take you up.

---

## Session Start-Up

We all go through difficult times. They come in many forms in many seasons. Divorce. Abandonment. Betrayal. Disappointment. A layoff. Sickness. I hope I'm not ruining your parade, but even Jesus said, "In the world you will have tribulation; but be of good cheer, I have overcome the world" (John 16:33). While we are guaranteed trouble in this life, we have good news: Jesus has overcome the world!

We can't choose what life will bring our way, but we can choose what happens in us as a result. We cast the role that trials will play in our lives. We can either let them take us in the direction of despair, depression and bitterness or we can use them to help grow in us deep roots in Jesus and bear the fruits of the Holy Spirit. It's up to us.

In times of difficulty, you will only be able to see acres of diamonds if you develop a dependence on God and get your attitude right. This does not happen overnight, nor does it happen on the outside. It happens over time, on the inside. You must believe and keep believing God. You must trust and keep trusting God. You must trade bitterness for joy and keep doing so. If your root system is going down, it's a matter of time before your fruit system starts bearing fruit up.

It's easy to get and stay negative when you can't see acres of diamonds. This is the enemy's desire for you. He wants you to believe that you have no choice but to quit. That you should leave where God has called you to stay because it's too hard. That you should let someone else fulfill the vision God has specifically given to you. For believers, negativism is not part of the plan. No kind of negative information—that we receive from others or think ourselves—has anything to do with the spirit God has called us to bear.

When the nation of Israel was close to reaching the Promised Land, Moses sent a group of spies to scout the land. It was amazing! Fertile. Flowing with milk and honey. Grapes so big it took two men to carry one bunch. Great news, right? Not quite. With the exception of Joshua and Caleb, the spies came back with a negative report. They told Moses and all the people of Israel that there were giants in the land who could not be defeated. "It's too hard; we can't do it." Joshua and Caleb disagreed. They were confident the Israelites could defeat the enemy and take the land God had promised them. But no one listened. Soon, the Israelites began to talk themselves out of the victory that God was ready to give them.

In order to be victorious, we must keep fighting against that spirit of negativism and live in hopeful expectation. There is undiscovered potential right before you. Even in your darkest hour, there is living water in Jesus Christ. The key to finding this diamond is to get anchored in Him. Don't focus on the negative report; focus on Jesus.

God promised He would be with us through every situation we face here on earth. He won't ever leave us. This should strengthen our faith.

We don't fall apart in the storm. Nor do we complain or give up. We take courage. We stand up on our two feet, fix our eyes on Jesus, and say, "I can make it through this storm. I am not quitting. I am going forward."

## Talk about It

How does your attitude affect your environment, personally and with others?

## Session 3 Video

*Watch video session 3. While viewing the video, use the outline and spaces below to record key ideas or any thoughts you want to remember.*

### Video Teaching Notes

It's not what happens *to* you that matters but what happens *in* you.

Your attitude is the deciding factor.

Nothing catches God by surprise.

If you let Him, He can turn your trial into fruit.

You can have peace in the midst of a storm.

Quit expecting the worst and get on your tiptoes in expectation.

"Now as the people were in expectation, and all reasoned in their hearts about John, whether he was the Christ or not . . ." (Luke 3:15). The New English Bible translates it "on the tiptoe of expectation."

A spirit of negativism will keep you out of your Promised Land.

Make a decision at your spiritual meristem line that you will not quit.

God will get you where He wants you to go, little by little.

### Video Discussion

Name one thing that struck you or that you learned, experienced or gained from this video teaching.

## Small-Group Discussion

1. There is an old saying, "The gem cannot be polished without friction, nor man perfected without trials." What does it take to mature as a Christian?

2. Many Christians never reach their full potential. In the video teaching and in *Acres of Diamonds*, I call these folks "bonsai Christians." No matter how long it has been since they first made the decision to trust in Jesus, they have not grown spiritually. They're stuck, getting snipped and cut on all sides from the enemy or just life itself. What has hindered your spiritual growth? How can you change this?

3. Ephesians 4:31–32 says, "Let all bitterness, wrath, anger, clamor, and evil speaking be put away from you, with all malice. And be kind to one another, tenderhearted, forgiving one another, even as God in Christ forgave you."

   Why is it important that we not harbor bitterness in our lives? What can we do instead?

4. In *Acres of Diamonds* (pp. 104–105), I tell the story of Shannen Wehunt, a woman who lost both of her children. She said, "I miss my kids terribly. There are times I drive past Yellow Creek Cemetery, where both of my children are buried, and I just cry and cry. But I keep trusting the Lord. I keep reminding myself He is good. I keep thanking Him for giving me the gift of two beautiful children who are now in His arms. I can't say I understand this. But I choose to trust the Lord, even when it's painful. Even when it's lonely. Even when I know I will never hear my kids call me 'Mama' on this earth. I trust God. He's all I've got."

   What does her statement say about the roots she grew deep in God? How can this encourage you?

5. In the video teaching, I encourage you to believe it's tiptoe time. We read in Luke 3:15–16,

   > Now as the people were in expectation, and all reasoned in their hearts about John, whether he was the Christ or not, John answered, saying to all, "I indeed baptize you with water; but One mightier than I is coming, whose sandal strap I am not worthy to loose. He will baptize you with the Holy Spirit and fire."

   The New English Bible translation says the people were not only in expectation, they were "on the tiptoe of expectation." Talk about the last time you were on the tiptoe of expectation.

6. In *Acres of Diamonds* (pp. 133–134) I write,

If you are a parent, it is your responsibility to make sure the spirit of negativism does not land on your marriage or on your children or in your home. If you are leading in the workplace, your responsibility is to make sure your department, staff or team does not get into a negative funk. If you are in any position of influence, great or small, you are responsible to guard that place from a spirit of negativism. Set the standard. Don't feed into criticism. Don't feed into finding fault. Don't feed into backbiting. Don't feed into complaining. Don't feed into whining.

Think about the influence you have in your everyday life. Who do you lead? How can you set the standard for a positive, hopeful and expectant attitude in your family, in your classroom, on your team or on your staff?

7. Have you ever anchored your faith in something or someone other than Jesus? If so, what was the end result?

## Bonus Questions

8. When we make good choices and maintain a right attitude in times of hardship, it can produce in us the fruits of the Spirit: "love, joy, peace, longsuffering, kindness, goodness, faithfulness, gentleness, self-control" (Galatians 5:22). Talk about a time of difficulty in your life in which you grew in your character. Which of these fruits was developed the most?

9. While the number one anchor we must have in this life is Jesus, it's also important to drop the anchors of purpose, courage, worship and the Church. Choose one of these four anchors and share how it has significantly impacted your life for the good.

10. When was the last time you felt God had promised something, yet the progress felt as though it was going way too slowly?

## Wrap-Up

Today we have learned that the biggest changes don't happen above ground, at least not at first. The work of cultivating spiritual growth begins underneath the soil. We must grow deep roots in Jesus and get anchored in Him so He can uncover acres of diamonds in our lives. While the process may unfold slowly, little by little, we can trust that He will finish the work that He started.

Let's close this time together in prayer. Here are some ideas from this session that can guide your conversation with God:

- Thank God for helping you grow spiritually as you work out your salvation, day in and day out.
- Ask Him to help you be a part of a remnant that will grow roots downward and bear fruit upward.
- Surrender any thoughts of bitterness and negativism and allow the Holy Spirit to fill you with joy unspeakable and hopeful expectation.
- Thank Him for His perfect timing and that His ways are greater than our ways. Confess your commitment to continue trusting in Him.

## Prepare for the Next Session

Before the group meets again, read chapter 9 in *Acres of Diamonds*.

# BETWEEN SESSIONS

## Personal Reflection

It is said that when Henry Wadsworth Longfellow was an old man, an admirer asked him how he was able to write so beautifully. Pointing to a nearby apple tree, the famous writer replied, "That apple tree is very old, but I never saw prettier blossoms on it than those it now bears. The tree grows a little new wood every year . . . and it is out of that new wood that the blossoms come. Like the apple tree, I try to grow a little new wood each year."[*]

Before you can grow to your full potential, achieve great heights and uncover the acres of diamonds God has planned for you, you must be firmly planted and rooted in faith in Jesus. It takes work to tend to your roots. Take time to study God's Word, communicate regularly with Him through worship and prayer, and commit to trusting in Him.

Reflect on the verses below. List five ways you can uncover acres of diamonds of spiritual growth. Then, commit to doing them.

Grow in the grace and knowledge of our Lord and Savior Jesus Christ.

2 Peter 3:18

Therefore, leaving the discussion of the elementary principles of Christ, let us go on to perfection, not laying again the foundation of repentance from dead works and of faith toward God.

Hebrews 6:1

Now the ones that fell among thorns are those who, when they have heard, go out and are choked with cares, riches, and pleasures of life, and bring no fruit to maturity. But the ones that fell on the good ground are those who, having heard the word with a noble and good heart, keep it and bear fruit with patience.

Luke 8:14–15

[*]J. W. Mahood, "Mental Health," *Epworth Herald*, February 5, 1910.

For this reason we also, since the day we heard it, do not cease to pray for you, and to ask that you may be filled with the knowledge of His will in all wisdom and spiritual understanding; that you may walk worthy of the Lord, fully pleasing Him, being fruitful in every good work and increasing in the knowledge of God.

Colossians 1:9–10

But also for this very reason, giving all diligence, add to your faith virtue, to virtue knowledge, to knowledge self-control, to self-control persever-ance, to perseverance godliness, to godliness brotherly kindness, and to brotherly kindness love. For if these things are yours and abound, you will be neither barren nor unfruitful in the knowledge of our Lord Jesus Christ.

2 Peter 1:5–8

## Personal Action

It's important to grow and work out your faith every day, even as storms rage. When trouble comes, drop the anchors of purpose, courage, worship and the Church. Choose one of these four areas that needs more attention. Perhaps you are so inundated with a challenge that you feel you can't see your purpose. Perhaps you have been so battered by a storm, you feel more afraid than brave. Perhaps you have disconnected with God and can't remember the last time you worshiped Him outside of a church service. Perhaps you have slacked off on getting fed spiritually in a local church.

Pick one area and commit to personal growth. List three steps you can take, starting now, to make this happen.

# ❖ 4 ❖

# Work Is Worship

---

**Big Idea for This Session**

God doesn't call everybody into full-time ministry. This doesn't mean He can't use those in the workplace to impact others for Christ. He does! In fact, His anointing can be just as great when believers carry their crosses into the marketplace.

---

## Session Start-Up

Sunday morning. It's church time. You settle into your seat, waiting to see what God will do. Maybe you're hungry. Maybe you're doubting. Maybe you're just worn out from the cares of the week. But as a melody emerges and voices commune in worship, your heart stirs under the presence of God. You begin soaking in the atmosphere of heaven, and you remember all the ways God has shown His goodness in the past week and before. Music fills your soul with joy, and, almost involuntarily, you raise your hands to worship God. *Sigh*. If only every day could be Sunday.

When Monday rolls around, things feel, well, different. Maybe you dread getting ready for another day on the job. Maybe you enjoy your work, but the people you work with bring you down. Maybe you're excited by what can happen in the office today, but your heart longs for the presence of the Lord you felt at church the day before. Why does Monday often feel different than Sunday?

Whatever you do for a living, I have very good news. God can use you in that place for His purpose. You can impact your work environment and shine your light for Jesus. The anointing of God is not reserved for those who preach on a stage. We often categorize full-time ministry in this capacity, but the truth is, if you are a believer, you are in full-time ministry. The next big revival will not come from a church platform; it will come in the workplace!

The majority of those who tune into our weekly broadcasts are not pastors by trade. Many of you would probably admit that the thought of preaching a sermon every week would be last on your bucket list. And that is okay! God has given you specific gifts, talents and skill sets for a specific reason. A pastor's role holds no more weight in the Kingdom of God than your role at work. Even the vast reach our ministry has been blessed with to influence others is nothing in comparison to the level of influence believers have in the workplace.

God values work just as much as He values ministry. Jesus worked as a carpenter until He was thirty years old and only then went into vocational ministry for three years. God could have sent Him into any family, but He chose a carpenter's home. Jesus himself was a hard worker in a hands-on job. May we not minimize this. When it came time for Him to carry the cross to His impending death, He didn't do so in secrecy. He trudged one step at a time through the marketplace. The marketplace! Exactly where you should be carrying your cross.

Your workplace is your place of influence. Could you imagine what this world would look like if anointed Christians started viewing their workplaces as pulpits? You don't have to preach a sermon or thump your Bible in someone's face. Small acts of kindness will open doors to share with someone the Good News. Approach your job activated by the power of the Holy Spirit. Even if you dislike your job, God can uncover acres of diamonds right where you are.

With God, there are no accidents, only divine ordinations. You are where you are for a very specific reason, and that reason is always souls. Keep being a light in this dark world. You can begin to change the world for Jesus one soul at a time.

## Talk about It

What does faith have to do with work? Discuss specific ways your faith has improved or affected your job performance or your relationship with your co-workers.

## Session 4 Video

*Watch video session 4. While viewing the video, use the outline and spaces below to record key ideas or any thoughts you want to remember.*

### Video Teaching Notes

The Hebrew word for work, *avodah*, means "work, worship and service."

Work is worship.

Work mattered to Jesus. Not only did 80 percent of the parables He taught have to do with the workplace, He worked as a carpenter.

The cross doesn't belong in the Church only; it also belongs in the marketplace.

The anointing is the anointing—whether it is on a preacher or a business person.

Big doors swing on little hinges.

Stand out in the workplace for having an excellent attitude and an excellent spirit.

Do what's expected and then some.

_____

_____

_____

"Arise, shine; for your light has come! And the glory of the LORD is risen upon you" (Isaiah 60:1).

_____

_____

_____

### *Video Discussion*

Name one thing that struck you or that you learned, experienced or gained from this video teaching.

## Small-Group Discussion

1. In the video teaching, I talk about work being equal with worship. How do you approach your job as worship?

2. Colossians 3:23–24 tells us, "And whatever you do, do it heartily, as to the Lord and not to men, knowing that from the Lord you will receive the reward of the inheritance; for you serve the Lord Christ."

    What are some ways that you have conducted yourself at work with the mindset of doing it "as to the Lord"?

3. In 2018 the Barna Group partnered with Abilene Christian University to produce a study on how faith is integrated at work.[*]

*Barna Group, "What Faith Looks Like in the Workplace," October 30, 2018, https://www.barna.com/research/faith-workplace/.

Most of the findings of the working Christians surveyed were encouraging:

- 82 percent believe that Christians should act ethically
- 74 percent believe that they should speak the truth
- 66 percent believe that they should make friends with non-Christians
- 59 percent believe that they should withstand temptation
- 58 percent believe that they should do excellent work in an effort to bring glory to God

When it came to the influence Christians should have in their places of employment, the numbers decreased significantly. For instance, only one third (35 percent) believe they should help mold the culture of their workplaces. And only one quarter (24 percent) believe sharing the Gospel is a responsibility. Reflect on these numbers.

Where do you fall in one or more of these categories? Do you believe you should shape the culture of your workplace? Why or why not?

4. In the video teaching, I discuss the importance of standing out on the job. How can you be a better example of Jesus where you work?

5. What are some of the challenges you face on the job?

6. In *Acres of Diamonds* ( pp. 144–145) I write,

> Did you know that of all of Jesus' parables, 80 percent of them had a workplace context? Did you know that of all of Jesus' public appearances recorded in the Bible, nearly all occurred in the marketplace? . . .
>
> Now think about this. Jesus was not born into a super religious family in the community, like that of a priest. God chose to send His Son into the home of a carpenter. A middle-class, blue-collar home . . . Jesus would stay in the

workforce with his father for at least twenty years before He would ever be released for the last three and a half years of his life into His ministry. The Son of God spent more time in the workforce than in ministry. Jesus was as much in the will and purpose of God when He was sawing wood, making tables and constructing chairs as He was when He was teaching, healing the sick and raising the dead.

Work matters! So much so that Jesus had a "regular" job, just like you. It wasn't beneath Him. In fact, it shaped who He was. How does this truth change your attitude about work?

7. We find a list of the fruits of the Spirit in Galatians 5:22–23: love, joy, peace, longsuffering, kindness, goodness, faithfulness, gentleness and self-control. Share a specific example of a time you allowed God to develop in you and grow one or more of these characteristics in the workplace.

## Bonus Questions

8. How important is the anointing of the Holy Spirit on your life when you begin your workday? How intentional are you in asking God to empower you? Why or why not?

9. What are some responsibilities or tasks in your job description that you may perceive to be without value, menial or unimportant? Do you slack off at times in these areas because they feel "less than"? How can you stand out for Jesus and execute them with excellence?

10. Describe a time in which you were able to influence your workplace culture in a positive and life-affirming way. What did the previous environment look like? How were you able to make a difference? What was the outcome?

## Wrap-Up

When we approach work as worship, we can find purpose. We can ask God to use us in whatever we do, even if it is not our dream job. Committing to excellence in this area pleases God. Some of you may work in an environment that is hostile to Christians or just plain stressful. When you are empowered with the anointing of the Holy Spirit, you can make a difference and uncover acres of diamonds even in such a place of heat and pressure.

Let's close this time together in prayer. Here are some ideas from this session that can guide your conversation with God:

- Thank God for providing you with employment (or thank Him that employment is coming).
- Ask Him to help you view your work as worship and to perform on the job with excellence and with a great attitude.
- Petition God to empower you with a special anointing of the Holy Spirit in the workplace and to develop in you the fruits of His Spirit so you can be equipped to serve others and point them to Jesus.
- Thank Him in advance for sending you opportunities in which you can help others on the job, encourage them through tough situations or share the love of Jesus with them.

## Prepare for the Next Session

Before the group meets again, read chapter 10 in *Acres of Diamonds*.

## Personal Reflection

The average American spends ninety thousand hours at work over his or her lifetime, but 87 percent of Americans have no passion for their jobs.[*] This tells me that most of us are grinding it out to get a paycheck and disliking every minute of it. Perhaps you can relate.

Here's the deal. Some of you may be lucky or blessed enough to enjoy the job of your dreams. Fact is, most of us aren't. But we do need to provide for our families. We need to pay the rent or the mortgage and put food on the table. Is it possible to find purpose and passion in employment that may not be satisfying? Absolutely!

An ancient prophet wrote the following:

> Arise, shine; for your light has come! And the glory of the LORD is risen upon you. For behold, the darkness shall cover the earth, and deep darkness the people; but the LORD will arise over you, and His glory will be seen upon you. The Gentiles shall come to your light, and kings to the brightness of your rising. Lift up your eyes all around, and see: They all gather together, they come to you; your sons shall come from afar, and your daughters shall be nursed at your side.
>
> Isaiah 60:1–4

*Gentiles* in this passage of Scripture refers to those who do not know God. Think about all the people you work with who are spiritually lost. Now think about the place of influence God has given you. *Arise and shine*. In other words, stand up and stand out. God does not want His people in a dark world hiding the light He has given them.

You may not love flipping hamburgers, selling shoes or supporting a sales team, but that might be the very place God has called you to. You are His acres of diamonds to the lost. If you're going to attract the attention of your co-workers for Jesus, stand up and stand out.

*Rachel Premack, "17 Seriously Disturbing Facts about Your Job," *Business Insider*, August 2, 2018, https://www.businessinsider.com/disturbing-facts-about-your-job-2011-2.

It's time to view your workplace as a mission field. Don't worry—for those of you who are shy in proclaiming your faith, I'm not talking about putting tracts in every cubicle or preaching to every person that enters the breakroom. I'm talking about being kind to others, using speech that edifies those around you, adding value by going over and beyond what your job description dictates and being diligent and excellent in the work you are given. Don't do these things just to make your boss or supervisor happy; do these things to please God. You know what else pleases God? Sharing the Good News of faith with others. If opportunities arise to encourage or even pray with someone, seize the moment. The time is now. Don't let moments pass you by in which you can change the course of someone's life for Jesus.

Give God the space to speak to your heart. Ask Him to bring to mind certain people you can minister to at work or specific ways to bring others closer to Him. Write these names down. Pray for them every day.

## Personal Action

Choose one thing this week—that you are not doing already—that will exemplify Jesus and please God where you are employed. Make it personal. For example, think of someone who is struggling in some area. Consider praying for or sharing the hope of Jesus with them. Will you be brave enough to possibly be the only example of Jesus this person might ever see? Will you be brave enough to uncover the acres of diamonds of salvation to someone in your workplace?

Or, think of your job performance. What can you do differently to please God and shine your light? How can you exemplify excellence? For instance, you can show up early, stay late or help another team member or department with a project that may not fall under your direct responsibility.

Write it down—then do it.

# How to Be a Hero

---

**Big Idea for This Session**

Underneath the craggy soil of family conflicts, pressures and temptations, God wants to uncover the diamonds of salvation, unity, victory, healing and love. Not just for you, but also for your spouse, your children and generations to come.

---

## Session Start-Up

God created a plan for companionship called marriage. He is the biggest supporter of your marriage. Family is also important to God. That's probably not news to you. But have you ever thought about just how important it is? The two most vital decisions you can make are to, one, trust Jesus as your Savior and, two, guide your family to do the same. It is not enough to secure your own place in eternity. God wants to save your entire family! "Believe on the Lord Jesus Christ, and you will be saved, you and your household" (Acts 16:31).

If we want to uncover acres of diamonds in those we love, we've got to set the standard and lead them to Jesus. One way to do this is to get planted in the house of God. Matthew 16:18 says, "I will build my church, and the gates of Hades shall not prevail against it." God is not just interested in individuals coming into His Church; He desires to see whole families worshiping together. Our spiritual growth can affect the spiritual development of our families. God delights in this. And in His book, it equals hero status.

If you lead your family to Jesus, then you're following the examples of the men and women listed in Hebrews 11, also known as the Faith Hall of Fame. These spiritual giants, including Gideon, David and Abraham, were ordinary people who did extraordinary things for God. Teach your family to know and serve Jesus and continually build their faith. You'll be a hero, a spiritual giant, in God's eyes.

I do not know how old your children are, or if you have any at all. I do know it's never too late to be a hero in your family. Now is the time. Decide today to be one. Your children are worth the fight. Your spouse, your parents, your estranged brother or sister . . . they are all worth praying for and believing in. Do not let guilt set in if you think you have failed in this area. It's not about what you have done or what you have not done. It's about doing all you can, starting now, to lead your loved ones to Jesus.

At times the battle can be fierce and your present circumstances may cause you to wonder if your family will ever be saved or healed or reconciled. During these times it is even more crucial not to give up. We may not be in total control, but God is. He has promised that if we continue to be obedient in fighting for our family, He will fight for us. Consider this: Instead of fighting *with* your spouse or your kids, start fighting *for* your family. His grace is sufficient to bring to light the diamonds of victory over strife, bitterness, infidelity, bickering and unforgiveness.

I realize that not all of you reading this participant's guide are married, have kids or have a traditional two-parent home. If this describes you, don't skip this session. You will still find nuggets of wisdom in these next few pages. If you're single, use this opportunity to learn from those who are or have been married in your group. If you are child-free, this session can help you guide a child you know or one you might consider mentoring.

## Talk about It

How has your relationship with God shaped your idea of marriage and family?

## Session 5 Video

*Watch video session 5. While viewing the video, use the outline and spaces below to record key ideas or any thoughts you want to remember.*

### Video Teaching Notes

Every family goes through times of intense heat and pressure.

If your neighbor's grass looks greener, you need to fertilize your own yard.

Be a hero to your family.

There's nothing greater than a family forgiving again, loving again, coming together again, trying again.

Fight for your family, your children, your home.

### Video Discussion

Name one thing that struck you or that you learned, experienced or gained from this video teaching.

## Small-Group Discussion

1. The enemy comes to steal, kill and destroy. Are there areas of conflict in your family that seem too overwhelming to conquer on your own? If so, talk about one.

2. It seems most of our calendars are slammed with events, appointments, schedules, reminders and to-dos. What are the top three most important things to you? Is family near the top of the list? If not, it should be! How do you make your family a priority? Do you need to reevaluate how and where you spend your time?

3. What habits have you instilled in your household to foster a faith-filled atmosphere? How can you practice these things consistently?

4. Every couple experiences conflict. If your relationship doesn't, you probably haven't been married long enough. It is only a matter of time before a relationship moves from the fairy-tale-like "in love" experience to a choice that takes commitment, effort and sacrifice—and that's worth it! Every couple I know struggles to maintain a connection and nurture growth in their relationship, especially with life challenges, mounting responsibilities and packed schedules. How do you choose what's best for you and your family in order to keep a healthy home?

5. Nurturing strong families is a must to make future disciples. If you can help a couple or a single parent get closer to God, you can influence multiple future generations. How do you encourage other couples or single parents as they endure tough seasons?

6. What are some distractions, lies or obstacles the enemy puts in place to prevent families and married couples from being united and serving God together? What can you do to prevent these things from happening in your own families?

7. What are some of the biggest sacrifices you have made for your marriage or your family? If you are not married and are child-free, what are some of the sacrifices your parents have made for you? Give an example of how it has paid off.

## Bonus Questions

8. The demands of work and ministry, a growing to-do list, financial challenges, lack of sleep, a surge in stress and anxiety and health problems can make it difficult to prioritize quality time with our loved ones. Give an example of how staying connected with those closest to you has improved your relationship.

9. In *Acres of Diamonds* (pp. 168–169) I write,

> When you dedicate your children to the Lord, you put them in a spiritual safehouse. Sometimes we need God to help us open our eyes to see the potential in our children. You may see your kid as sweet or shy, impulsive or studious, rebellious or obedient, but God sees them in a completely different light. He sees them as weapons.
>
> Behold, children are a heritage from the LORD, the fruit of the womb is a reward. Like arrows in the hand of a warrior, so are the children of one's youth. Happy is the man who has his quiver full of them; they shall not be ashamed, but shall speak with their enemies in the gate.
>
> Psalm 127:3–5

> When God saved you, He did not just think of *you* being saved. He also saw in you another generation, and another generation, and another generation that He would save. It's never just about you. When God looks at us, He sees multi-generational beings. The acres of diamonds of spiritual blessing can extend far beyond our own lives on earth.

How can you see children as weapons to bring forth hope, healing and salvation for future generations?

10. How does God help us with the struggles we face in our families?

## Wrap-Up

Today we have learned that being married and having a family are not easy. Okay, I know, this is not breaking news. Unmet expectations, demanding responsibilities, challenging family dynamics and a fast-paced, busy lifestyle make it difficult to see the beauty, joy and wonder in those we love the most. But when we make the sacrifices, when we stay faithful, when we get plugged in to the local church and when we take the time to worship, we dig wells that will bring forth living water.

Let's close this time together in prayer. Here are some ideas from this session that can guide your conversation with God:

- Thank God that He desires to uncover acres of diamonds in your marriage and in your family. Ask Him to open your eyes to uncover areas of growth and areas of victory.
- Ask God to transform you by His power and to help you become the person, the parent or the spouse that He has called you to be. Ask Him to forgive you for the areas in which you have failed.
- Decree that no weapon formed against you or your family will prosper.
- Thank God for fighting for you and your loved ones, particularly if you are going through a tough season. Thank Him in advance for sending peace during the storm.

## Prepare for the Next Session

Before the group meets again, read chapters 11 and 12 in *Acres of Diamonds*.

## BETWEEN SESSIONS

### Personal Reflection

No matter what your marital status or family dynamic, God wants to uncover acres of diamonds in this field. The enemy does not want to see your family flourish with love, joy, devotion and faith. On the contrary, he wants to destroy them. Here's the good news: You are totally incapable of making it to the finish line of faith without the help of your Father in heaven. Yes, that's right—this is good news! It should take some pressure off. The best news is that He is willing and able to help you.

Think about some of the tough places in which you desperately need God's help. What are the acres of diamonds you want Him to uncover in your loved ones? Salvation? Recovery from an addiction? Peace from mental or emotional oppression? Make a list of three of them below. Then spend time in prayer and open yourself to receiving God's Spirit to help you and your family make it to the finish line.

## Personal Action

In *Acres of Diamonds* (pp. 160–161) I talk about how Abraham had once built wells for himself and his family:

> The Middle Eastern climate is hot and dry. Digging wells was hard, putting it mildly. There were no drills or machines around to make the process more efficient. It required blood, sweat, tears and a lot of time. When Abraham dug those wells, he understood that the time and the energy he invested in digging were not just for him and his wife. They were for his son and for generations to follow. This reminds me of the Scripture, "A good man leaves an inheritance to his children's children" (Proverbs 13:22). This doesn't just mean money or the house; this is a spiritual inheritance that is eternal.
>
> When Abraham died, the Philistines filled the wells with dirt. The water still flowed under the surface, but there was no way for it to come out. The enemy thought they could drive the next generation out without this source of water. But Isaac, Abraham's son, was willing to fight for the well. Some wells are worth fighting over. If you are in a low place today, if your marriage is on the rocks, if your children are not living for God, if strife and contention are consuming the atmosphere of your home, know this: You are closer to the water than ever before.

I offer four wells that you can begin to dig, starting today, to find God's best for you and your family and generations to come:

- The well of sacrifice
- The well of discipline
- The well of quality time
- The well of faithfulness

Under each of these four categories, list two things you can do to dig these wells.

## Well of Sacrifice

## Well of Discipline

*Well of Quality Time*

_____

_____

_____

_____

_____

_____

_____

_____

_____

*Well of Faithfulness*

_____

_____

_____

_____

_____

_____

_____

_____

_____

# ❖ 6 ❖

# Live Now in the Light of Eternity

> **Big Idea for This Session**
>
> No matter how devastating your current situation, you, right now, are standing on top of acres of diamonds. Jesus is your victory. He has already provided you with a way out of what may seem impossible. And when life is hard, know that He has also promised you the gift of eternal life with Him in heaven. Your eternal home will make everything you go through on earth worth it!

## Session Start-Up

Conflict brings strength. Often we pray for God to get us out of a tough situation, and we get discouraged when He doesn't. But our Father in heaven knows something we don't. He knows that when we endure through the conflicts, we become strong enough to defend the very thing God wants to give us.

You see, God has already equipped you to win! If your situation seems impossible right now, know that you serve the God of the impossible.

Is there a hopeless situation in your life today? Be encouraged. God can breathe life into it. Your hopes may be dead and your dreams buried, but God can bring them to life, even in a new way. The prophet Ezekiel once stood in a valley of dead, dry bones. That's about as bad as it gets, right? Then something amazing happened. God said to the prophet,

> "Prophesy to the breath, prophesy, son of man, and say to the breath, 'Thus says the Lord GOD: "Come from the four winds, O breath, and breathe on these slain, that they may live."'" So I prophesied as He commanded me, and breath came into them, and they lived, and stood upon their feet, an exceedingly great army.
>
> Ezekiel 37:9–10

Your greatest victory can come when it seems as though everything around you is dead! Any time you see a man or woman enjoying success in God's Kingdom, there is a good chance they've been through the valley of devastation, hurt and rejection. It was after he had been thrown out of the city, stoned and left for dead that Paul spoke of being taken up into the third heaven and experiencing things too wonderful to speak of on earth (see 2 Corinthians 12:2–4). It was after John was exiled to a penal colony in Patmos that he penned the words, "I was in the Spirit on the Lord's Day, and I heard behind me a loud voice, as of a trumpet" (Revelation 1:10). As a result, John wrote the book of Revelation.

The psalmist said, "For in the time of trouble . . . He shall hide me; He shall set me high upon a rock. And now my head shall be lifted up above my enemies all around me; . . . I will sing, yes, I will sing praises to the LORD" (Psalm 27:5–6). When it feels as if you are in the valley of the shadow of death, glorify God. Thank Him in advance of your victory. See how He will use what the devil intended to harm you for good.

The battle is real! We need to suit up and fight. Paul talked about engaging in a spiritual war with the weapons of prophecy. Stay with me, here—don't let this trip you up. Prophecy is a word from God about your future. Though there are a number of ways God speaks to us, the most obvious is through the Bible. The Word of God is ripe with promises that we can use to prophesy over our lives. As we speak the prophetic word, our thoughts change and, in turn, so do our actions. Where you are may look nothing like acres of diamonds, but when you fight a spiritual battle with prophecy, armed with what God says in His Word, you have faith that one day it will.

How do you go to war with a prophecy? Decree what God says in the Bible. Say it out loud. Pray it. Speak what has been spoken over you, and God will fight with and for you.

> For the weapons of our warfare are not carnal but mighty in God for pulling down strongholds, casting down arguments and every high thing that exalts itself against the knowledge of God, bringing every thought into captivity to the obedience of Christ.
>
> 2 Corinthians 10:4–5

When the hand of the Lord is on your life, the prophecy is not guilt, condemnation and defeat. The prophecy over you is freedom, breakthrough and deliverance. You may be just one proclamation away from victory!

Life can be difficult. At any given time, there are precious people strained and stretched to their limit emotionally. There are people struggling with physical pain or pressured by financial difficulties. There are people challenged by disharmony and chaos in their families and their marriages. These things are part of the tapestry of life on earth. Our enemy wants us to focus on the temporary, the tough season we're in, and lose sight of the eternal. We become dangerous to his plans when we set our hearts on what will have an eternal impact. The devil does not want us to remember we are headed for heaven. But for those who believe in Jesus, we are!

Heaven is a real place. Jesus Himself said that His Father was preparing a place in heaven for all who trust Him. He even said that if it weren't true, He would tell us.

Believe it—heaven is real.

This world is not our final destination. It is not our true home. Our home is with our Father in heaven. If you have lost a loved one and you're suffering through unbearable pain and grief, get eternity on your mind. One glorious day the grave is going to burst wide open and death is going to be swallowed up in victory. This is powerful! And this is a promise for you if you believe in Jesus as your Lord and Savior.

## Talk about It

How often do you think about heaven in light of what you go through on earth?

## Session 6 Video

*Watch video session 6. While viewing the video, use the outline and spaces below to record key ideas or any thoughts you want to remember.*

### Video Teaching Notes

If we believe the Bible, our ultimate acres of diamonds is heaven.

"For the Lord Himself will descend from heaven with a shout, with the voice of an archangel, and with the trumpet of God. And the dead in Christ will rise first. Then we who are alive and remain shall be caught up together with them in the clouds to meet the Lord in the air. And thus we shall always be with the Lord. Therefore comfort one another with these words" (1 Thessalonians 4:16–18).

"In My Father's house are many mansions; if it were not so, I would have told you. I go to prepare a place for you. And if I go and prepare a place for you, I will come again and receive you to Myself; that where I am, there you may be also. And where I go you know, and the way you know" (John 14:2–4).

Heaven is real.

"For our light affliction, which is but for a moment, is working for us a far more exceeding and eternal weight of glory" (2 Corinthians 4:17).

Get heaven on your mind.

The greatest victory that Jesus ever won was won in a graveyard.

"The hand of the LORD came upon me and brought me out in the Spirit of the LORD, and set me down in the midst of the valley; and it was full of bones" (Ezekiel 37:1).

When the hand of the Lord is upon you, you can do the impossible.

"And Jabez called on the God of Israel saying, 'Oh, that You would bless me indeed, and enlarge my territory, that Your hand would be with me, and that You would keep me from evil, that I may not cause pain!' So God granted him what he requested" (1 Chronicles 4:10).

### Video Discussion

Name one thing that struck you or that you learned, experienced or gained from this video teaching.

## Small-Group Discussion

1. What are some things you will find in heaven? What are some things you won't find there?

2. When the apostle Paul knew it was time to die, he said,

> I have fought the good fight, I have finished the race, I have
> kept the faith. Finally, there is laid up for me the crown of
> righteousness, which the Lord, the righteous Judge, will give
> to me on that Day, and not to me only but also to all who
> have loved His appearing.
>
> 2 Timothy 4:7–8

It was obvious that Paul did not fear death. On the contrary, he
was filled with anticipation. He knew that when his life on earth
was over, he would be with the Lord and receive his reward—a
crown of righteousness. Paul declared that he had fought hard and
that he had overcome. Are you afraid to die? Why or why not?

3. In *Acres of Diamonds* ( p.194) I write,

> Heaven is a real place filled with wonders beyond what we
> can even begin to imagine. If you try to think of the greatest,
> most joy-filled and pleasurable place, it will not come close to
> what heaven will actually be like. God loves you. He prepared
> heaven for you, and He wants you to spend eternity there.

How does the truth of heaven's existence motivate or shape
what you do on earth for Jesus today?

4. What does the phrase *the hand of the Lord* mean to you? How
have you experienced the hand of the Lord upon your life? Talk
about it.

5. Jesus challenged His disciples with this simple exhortation:
"Nothing will be impossible for you" (Matthew 17:20). Impossible situations and impossible dreams are awesome because
they trigger the supernatural, miraculous power of God. If you
are facing something impossible, don't despair—this is God's
specialty. Talk about a current situation in which you need His
intervention. How does the Scripture above encourage you?

6. In *Acres of Diamonds* (p. 183) I write,

> The Word of God will get you where the will of God wants
> to take you. But you have to say it. You have to speak it. You
> have to declare it. You have to pray it. You have to decree it.

> God wants His followers to go to war using prophecy and declaring blessings for the future. Talk about the last time you held on
> to a promise found in the Bible. How did it help you walk through
> a tough time?

7. Have you ever experienced the presence and power of God in
an impossible situation? What was the outcome?

## Bonus Questions

8. In 1 Timothy 1:18–19, Paul writes, "This charge I commit to you,
son Timothy, according to the prophecies previously made
concerning you, that by them you may wage the good warfare,
having faith and a good conscience." How can you engage in
spiritual warfare by using biblical promises?

9. Hebrews 4:12 tells us,

> For the word of God is living and powerful, and sharper than
> any two-edged sword, piercing even to the division of soul
> and spirit, and of joints and marrow, and is a discerner of the
> thoughts and intents of the heart.

> How do these powerful characteristics of the Bible encourage
> you?

10. How do you think you will respond when you see Jesus
face-to-face?

## Wrap-Up

I hope you have been encouraged to know that whatever you are facing, if you're in it, you can win it! You serve a God of the impossible who can move heaven and earth for you. You also serve a God of eternity. He has prepared for you a home in heaven. The promise of spending eternity with Him is real. So live now and live well. And get eternity on your mind. Nothing you do on earth will be wasted if you do it with an eternal purpose.

Let's close this time together in prayer. Here are some ideas from this session that can guide your conversation with God:

- Thank Him for the reviving, healing breath of His Word and the promises that you can use to wage war for your future and future generations.
- Ask Him to put His hand upon your life so you can be a blessing to others and further His Kingdom.
- Thank God for the precious and priceless gift of salvation and the promise He gives of eternal life with Him.
- Ask the Holy Spirit to remind you of your purpose on earth and for you to live each day with that in mind.

## Personal Reflection

Ezekiel introduced the miracle of the dry bones coming alive by saying, "The hand of the LORD came upon me and brought me out in the Spirit of the LORD" (Ezekiel 37:1).

It's important to be in the Spirit. This isn't something weird or scary. All it means is getting in a rhythm of allowing Him to lead and speak to you. When you are in step with the Holy Spirit, you are open to His prompting. You are in tune with what God is doing.

When you are empowered by the Holy Spirit, the hand of the Lord comes upon you—and when it does, it is to do a specific thing. This is important: It is to accomplish a purpose in God's Kingdom. Here are three things you need to know about the hand of the Lord:

- *The blessing of the hand of the Lord is always connected to an assignment.* Never think that God's overall intention is to make you comfortable. We are created to be channels through which God can impact the world. His hand is not upon you to make you rich or popular. His hand is upon you to fulfill an assignment that has an eternal purpose.
- *The hand of the Lord is upon us to help, encourage and minister to people in low places.* When the hand of God came upon Ezekiel, God set him down in a valley. We aren't always blessed merely to enjoy a mountaintop experience; at times we are taken to a low place so we can see, really see, the people who are in this same place. And we are to make a difference in their lives by offering them a lifeline in Jesus. Make no mistake: God can be glorified in the low places of our lives just as much as He is on the mountaintop.
- *We cannot fail when the hand of the Lord is upon us.* I have experienced times when the hand of the Lord came upon me to fulfill an assignment that I, in my own strength and abilities, would fail at. Success came by way of Him alone. When the hand of the Lord is on you, you can do things that other people can't do. Nothing can stop you. Critics can't stop you. The enemy can't

75

stop you. A lack of money can't stop you. It's because God gives you His power to do whatever He has called you to do. This is unstoppable power!

Spend time in prayer right now. Ask God for His hand to be upon your life. Pray what Jabez prayed: "Oh, that You would bless me indeed, and enlarge my territory, that Your hand would be with me, and that You would keep me from evil, that I may not cause pain!" (1 Chronicles 4:10).

Ask God to give you opportunities in which you can encourage someone in a low place, bring glory to His name or further the Kingdom in some way. Write down what you feel God is speaking to your heart.

## Personal Action

If heaven is real, it's obvious that death is real. We are all appointed a time to die, to leave this earth. The truth that eternity in heaven awaits you should be encouraging! It should also give you a sense of urgency to share the Good News with those who do not know Jesus.

The responsibility of sharing the message of hope is entrusted to every believer. You included. There are unbelievers who may never hear the truth of Jesus Christ if you do not bring it to them. When you share the hope of Jesus, invite someone to church or tell them about your faith, you're planting a seed. God has entrusted you with His hope, His Word and His story, and He has positioned you on that path for such a time as this. You may never know what will lie on the other side of your obedience. Think about this—where would you be today if someone had not shared God's story with you?

You may say you follow Jesus, but if you are not compelled to share His love, it is time to reevaluate what you truly believe. This may feel a bit out of your comfort zone, but today ask the Lord to reveal to you who needs to encounter His love. You may very well have unbelievers in your direct circle of influence, such as in your workplace or community. Start there. Share the hope, peace and joy of the Good News with someone this week. And don't make it a one-time deal. Turn it into a lifestyle!

**Jentezen Franklin** is the senior pastor of Free Chapel, a multicampus church. Each week his television program, *Kingdom Connection*, is broadcast on major networks all over the world. A *New York Times* bestselling author, Jentezen has written numerous books, including *Acres of Diamonds*; *Love Like You've Never Been Hurt*; the groundbreaking *Fasting*; *Right People, Right Place, Right Plan* and *Fear Fighters*.

Jentezen and his wife, Cherise, have been married more than thirty years. They have five children and a growing number of grandchildren and make their home in Gainesville, Georgia.